to Patr

CW00502565

Before we B

with all good wishes,

Jackie Biggs

Jackie

Poems n Pints
4.5.21

Littoral Press

First published in 2021 by:
The Littoral Press, 15 Harwood Place,
Lavenham, Sudbury, Suffolk CO10 9SG

©Jackie Biggs

ISBN 978-1-912412-31-0

British Library Cataloguing-in-Publication Data: A catalogue record of this book is available from The British Library

All rights reserved

Printed and bound in Great Britain by:
4Edge Ltd. Hockley, Essex
www.4edge.co.uk

The Sibyl, with frenzied mouth uttering things not to be laughed at,
unadorned and unperfumed,
yet reaches to a thousand years with her voice.
Heraclitus, 5th century BC.

Acknowledgements

Grateful acknowledgement is made to the editors of the following magazines and online journals where some of these poems first appeared: *ASP Literary Journal, Visual Verse, The Dawntreader, Words for the Wild, Algebra of Owls, Three Drops from a Cauldron, As Above So Below, The Beach Hut,* The Being Human Project (Cultural Institute, Swansea University).

Also by Jackie Biggs:

The Spaces in Between, Pinewood Press, 2015
Breakfast in Bed, Indigo Dreams Publishing, 2019

Contents

Before we Breathe

Sibyl

She come

here now

new voice

from under waves

weaving words

with salt

soil

stone

The woman at the beach

Green waterproof coat flapping
woolly hat crammed,
she leans on her stick on the shoreline
while she gazes across the sea.
Every day she treks across the sand
splashing her wellies in frothy surf.
She doesn't know what she seeks,
but she's always looking.

Maybe she wants just to be there
to feel the breeze on her face
taste salt, scent seaweed, to breathe.
She studies the constancy – how waves build, rise and curl
endlessly coming and coming again, swash and backwash,
every seventh the biggest swell,
the longest reach.
She's always looking.

She rejoices in each moment when the sea pulls away –
that space behind the wave
how it holds peace in its waiting
before it builds and crests again.
On quiet grey days she loves the steely shine on the surface,
watches reflections of cold light on every little comber,
and her eyes track rippled mercury as it spreads for miles.
Always looking.

She ponders how to write the lines to illustrate that silvered joy,
but she does not find the words she needs.
She walks the long length of sand
peering down,
sometimes picks up a stone
or turns one with her foot.
Occasionally she'll pocket one,
if it's a perfect one.
Still looking

She wonders too at strata in rocks
how cliffs became massive blocks of slate,
giant black cubes
stacked and packed.
Then she will raise her eyes to the wide sky,
can she see the Llyn today?
She'll note the curve of horizon, consider the blue,
watch how clouds move.

Where I come from

Many farback years
deep under ocean
down in dark
only other creatures bring light

no sun there
where I come from, me.

Beasts swim with wings
glow-tentacles reach out
jelly-skirts pulse
fins make flashbright beams.

If no beings, no light
only black, see nothing
but fish
fish
they glow

where I come from

Transformation

leaving oceans below
we climb out of flowing waves
breathe air   grow limbs
traverse some in-between space
where we swim from sea towards sky

from green through blue shadow
we seek earthfall
we are jade
we will find a new way
and we will bring you pearls

Landfall

Exposed, scared, emerging first time from sea
onto shifting sand. Try to stand.
Worse than bad dream when you see yourself naked
on big beach and all others wear clothes and stare,
skinned like rabbit on a spit,
furless. Vivid flesh, muscles tight over bones.
Want to run back, let ocean fold me in herself again.
But that way closed.
New skin begin. Slowly spread on my raw body
from belly to limbs, to fingers and toes,
creep over breasts and neck to face, grow over all of me.
Don't know how long I stay, watching this cover form.
Maybe many days. And with skin, grows knowing.
Me sure ... must leave my sea for all time.

The visitor

Me nearly miss it down on sand.
Body, half buried
jaw split, fat paw awkward
broken back to body

little fingers, tufts and fur
long claws, flippers almost gone
odd bones around,
black hole where stomach

and another on back head.
All desiccated.
Wind warm from south,
white feather, small-slight

drifts up, makes arc
floats over seal pup.
Next day, tide move her.
ribs show, skull exposed, teeth.

Now facing sea
stripped paws set
ready-push.

Hollow eyes follow tide
receding far.
Maybe she go tomorrow

How she calls

She thirsts for me
and she calls,

whispers my name –
            come dance,

sometimes loud –
            come dive,

sometimes soft –
            come breathe.

Lapping with little splashings
to suggest, persuade,

she draws the undertow
so I feel the overthrow

arriving and departing
leaving and returning,

spreading her susurration
far away and close by

turn by turn
tide by tide

surge and suck,
pull in, *come swim,*

            dance in me,
so calls the mother sea.

Cantre'r Gwaelod

(The lost land of Wales, in Cardigan Bay)

Down along the deep causeways ancient voices still call
over sunken villages, bells toll from castle towers
above drowned ramparts and over-run dykes,
all swept away in a tide-swipe.

In the cool dark at the bottom of the bay
all I hear is whalesong calling over miles,
punctuated with dolphin clicks of greeting,
as a bottle-nose nudges gently from the side.

In the kind of sunlight you can only know here,
a reflection refraction shafts through fathoms
to tumblestones of seabed, where anemones linger.
Here is calmness in swamped cottage gardens

where pink corallina now bends its fronds,
golden brown tendrils of carragheen float
furbellow fingers reach out to stroke
my drifting body. And bells toll the unseen hour.

I am water

When sun is harsh in afternoon
I kneel, scoop up cool water
in cupped palms.

How fresh and full in throat,
going down. I pull it in,
feel cleanness, greenness
fill all cells in body.

And lake reaches
sucks me into itself
folds my heart in its currents,
where somehow I breathe,
move freely, and wonder

Where I come from,
where I will go.

Swim wild, allow lake to swallow me
into its peace.
Tiny fish flicker silver around naked flesh.
Water murmurs secret stories,
makes music flow over body
and into me.

My beginning and ending,
place of depart and return,
to and fro
lapping the shore
sipping me
wanting me more.

Where I come from,
where I will go.

Witches cauldron

Her green light shines out
through the arch in the undercliff,
a jade glimmer as sun rises into the day.
Her voice whispers your name
and resonates in the hollow,
accompanied by steady rhythm
of waves hitting foreshore
and the bellow and boom of seals.

She welcomes you into the swelling pool
where sea stirs to lift you towards open sky,
where it holds you and lets go.
Spend a day with her among
the folding magma of rock
in the echo of receding caves
and in the surge and suck of surf.

Evening sealight through the low arch
glows copper with diamond edges,
calls swimmers out again to the wide ocean.
You know it will soon be too late to go.

But linger a while,
rest in the lapping of the flood,
watch darkness fall and tide rise,
sealight dim to violet
as she murmurs

stay, stay, stay…

See the cup of the pool hold all the sky,
and you can swim among stars.

The ship

Ship come in dark
show no light
hear big-rattle
anchor chain
new moon setting.
Me see only faint outline
small dark ship.

Put out fire, too bright,
need to stay secret
not see me
keep safe
not want company.

A splash,
man swim to beach.
Me wait.
He lie on sand
breathe hard.

He wait.
Dawn come, him still there.
I brew tea
take tea, oatcake to man.

Lucky him, rest above tideline,
still sleep.
I sit, wait.
Ship all black, turns on anchor chain.
No flag. Me no read, but no letters on side.

He wakes.
Beard, very brown skin, many wrinkles,
white hair. More years than me?
Big fear in eyes.

Push oatcakes and tea to him,
move back.

He swallow food and drink fast.
No chew. Nods.
He smell of fish, bad fish, maybe dead seagull near.
Me nod back.
He sleep again.

Pick up cup
walk back to cave, my cave.
Only me.
Stew fish, make big soup,
cook flatbread.
Take food to beach.

No man. No ship. Nothing on sea.
Still smell dead thing,
seagull maybe.
Where he sleep,
skull on sand.

Two long bones, crossed.

Overlapping margins

Where you don't know
if you are on shore or at sea
surf can take you
suck you, carry, or dump you.

On that strand
between the spring and the neap
where sand shines in sunlight
the surge pushes, pulls,
shifts tonnes of stone in a day.

When seagulls glide above,
shining like lacewings
against the deep space of
forget-me-not-forever blue,
you heart fills.

Thundering waves smash into hard grit.
Earth and ocean shove and heave.
And as spindrift flies on the wind
your heart empties

and suddenly
there is no past, no future,
yet nothing stays the same.

Aurelia aurita

Moon jellies bump gently
against my body

as I float in flooding tide
early morning, late spring.

Creatures without brain
blood, eyes, or heart

yet beautiful free swimmers
pulsing movers

alive in their own light, iridescent silk,
with violet ornaments, carnal signals.

We let the sea swallow us
and drift together

while they murmur untold stories,
older than dinosaurs.

Before we breathe

I am *Atargatis*, or call me *Daesura*,
born among greenweeds,
merewif, sirenia.

I drift in amniotic silver ...
my place of beginning,
of birthing and holding

among seapeople
in hidden caverns
close to the bed of the ocean

where tide pulls me to itself
in cyanic currents.
I am *Aycayia, siyokoy*

ningyo, Pania of the Reef.
See my world ...
Light beams sink from far above

through luminescence,
sea sparkle saturated by moon
shimmers on greenflakes.

I am *merrow, melusine*
mami-water, maneli,
feel my world ...

Silky water cool-touches over skin
flows easy over scales.
I flick my tail and rise through fathoms

effortless, hydrodynamic.
I am *ben-varrey, La Sirene,*
kulilto, derketo, fishwoman.

Hear my world ...
I sing with my sisters,
our harp song riffles through waves

among mantra calls of whales,
echo-music of dolphins.
We hold the secrets of the sea

dream before we breathe,
before we see light
we gleam like gems in the deep.

Sirens

Those harpies,
they sing their songs all day long,
magical harmonies
like no sound ever heard before.
They sing to lure in men
and then
they leave them die.

What for?
For fun, the siren call goes on.
Serenade them in, entice them down
have their pleasure,
leave them die,
on and on,
that is the siren's song,
the only way they know.

They keep up their singing
day after day
day after night.
Everyone wants to hear
the sound of the siren,
and still to live;
but who is asking: Why is it
they sing at all,
why tempt sailors
into the deep and leave them die?

And who ever wonders
what will be the last sound
that *they* will hear?

Leopard seal as my lover

He is long, muscular and sleek
with a silver-dark pelt slicked all down his back,
wide smile with even teeth
framed by neat whiskers.
I lose myself in his big soft eyes,
liquid angel love.

How he turned that penguin inside out
flayed it ready to eat;
how strong he is,
and oh, his grace, his speed.

He sings to me over miles,
long ghostly moans
entertain me for hours and days;
and then, he is silent for so long
I fear he has gone away,
until little trills of melody arrive to surprise.

We are ice lovers, lingering on floes
among creaking walls during the longest days.
Until the pup comes,
then he'll be off, leave me to it.
Until I hear his haunting long distance song again ...
and I   melt.

Reflection

Earth of light
sky of earth
(from 'Dancing the Siguiriya', by Federico Garcia Lorca)

The sky is on the beach,
all the blue heavens are there at our feet.
Still and silent on a winter-weathered strand,
earth and space have contrived to meet.
The entire sky is shining on the sand,
there before us, spread all across the ground.
The world is upside down,
someone turned it all around.

Someone turned it all around,
the world is upside down.
There before us, spread all across the ground,
the entire sky is shining on the sand.
Earth and space have contrived to meet,
still and silent on a winter-weathered strand,
all the blue heavens are there at our feet.
The sky is on the beach.

Drowning islands

People are buzzing in the cafes
over iced coffees, fresh water, whirring fans,
hubbub stokes the temperature
until noise scalds my brain.

There is a wind getting up
making dust bunnies in the sand
stings of heat hopping about, hitting bare legs
with pinpricks of fire,

even the breeze has heat on its leading edge
the sky is aflame.
Heavy air pushes me down,
my head aches, there's a storm coming.

Silence would be serene,
with a little touch of cool sea-swelling
pulling the slack into quiet
settling around my body.

Storm or no, I dive in,
swim under for moments,
deeper and deeper, as long as I can …
and when I rise to breathe

I look towards shore
the village in a haze of heat
behind vision blurred with brine
as salt water fills my eyes

and the last thing I see
is the island
disappearing
as sea rises

Breaking the surface

Sickle fins cut ocean calm
        rise and dip
                rise and dip

two   three   four   five
        arcing through sealight
polished skin in spindrift

leaping over waterbeams

        we are here, we are here
                come play
                        come play

make seaweed sail
        see jellyfish fly

snapping jaws slapping tails

        smiley faced bottlenoses
chuckle in sunshine.

Mother and calf rise and dive
        rise and dive

                follow them down

hear her whistle
        as she calls her name through oceans

        I am here

                I am here
                        come play

come play

geigercounter giggle

clicktick tickclick

clickclick clickclick clickclick

finding friends in sound patterns
cackles snickers

never silent

always shows her joy

grins from eye to eye.

Bouquet by the beach

Wet wool hangs raw from barbs on a fence
where the smell of sheep had gathered

ferns uncurl in woods to hide bluebells,
their fragrance sketched all over the air.

A thousand flowers of hawthorn open,
tiny stamens like dots of dust

on a perfect white cloth.
On cliffs where water falls sea pinks hug slate,

thrift in abundance, overlaying
seaweed traces on a breeze.

Salt stings your lips, ties knots in your hair,
tickles your nose, fills your head.

In the café a caramel cookie rests
wide and flat, sweet and delicate in its thinness,

on a bone china plate; fragments of chocolate
soften in the sun,

and there is coffee. Breathe through the steam,
catch scents of chocolate, of bluebells, and the sea.

Low tide

On the farthest beach at the lowest tide
cliffs high as sky lean over.

Look up to towers of granite grey
strata of centuries carved into giant cubes,
stacked and packed
blocks of ancient power.

Look up
to where buzzards drift
in silent circles
floating away the day

and topple under the weight
of ... upside down
vertigo.

Turn to the tide
flattest sea-soft sands
waves of bubbling surf
glittering on the sunshine ebb.

Returning

For now at last I know
That there is no escape
(Alun Lewis, 'The Sentry')

For how do you learn how to breathe again
after years of holding?
Your mind full of brown mud and shit
you stand by the cliff edge
among an abundance of thrift.

The mass of pink splits your brain like a mortar shell,
lightning strikes your heart
so hard it burns ventricles.

For you have longed for this moment –
clear sky, fresh sea air.

Breathe in   hold   breathe out   pause   repeat.

Your nose and ears still clogged with dirt and dust
but you hear the roar of waves below
over the bombardment that echoes in your head.

Salty brine of Irish Sea air penetrates
the fog of gas and stink of the rotten trench
as you remember waiting to scramble over.

Smoke and barbed wire, the bullet hail attack,
bloody limbs flying, brains and guts scattered.

in   hold   out   pause   repeat.

Shouts and screams.
Your mates' eyes staring up
through drifting ochre smoke.

Nothing looks at nothing.

Life is finished
tears rain all down your face.

You peer over the edge
red rocks pummelled by surf froth far below,
as blood bubbles from a blown-apart throat.

How do you come home?
Will this wide open space sometime bring peace?

Breathe in   hold   breathe out   pause   repeat.

How do you learn to live again?
Remember to breathe freely?
If you want to keep breathing.

For the pinks are only grey, the sky steel,
the sea rutted iron, the path a trench.
And death lives in you.

Breathe in   hold   breathe out   pause

Memory is held by the water

they sit on the wall of the old town bridge
        that place of endless departures
below the high castle walls

usually men   mostly at night
        they are silent unseen

this one is young
        his white face looks down between
black boots as his legs dangle

he will enter me soon   or walk away

when he slips in I will hold him close
        but I will not interfere
as he sinks into my depths

I will feel him among my green weeds
        and in my vortices

carry him in undercurrents

with migrating salmon
        over the silt and mud of my bed
to the sea and out on the full tide

as all the other lads before him
        over countless centuries.

I never know why they choose me
        maybe because I am dark and very cold

there is certainty in my currents and eddies

no chance for a change of mind
          bitter as brine

I am always here

yet I flow forever   east to west

tidal   so they are sure

          I will carry their cargo

          take all their weight.

Skin

A tiny sip of lichen slips
	through skin
	and creeps slow towards her wrist.

Algae emerge
	from the purlicue web,
	epidermis writhes into green

between the index and the next finger.
	Moss extends over the backs of her hands,
	a soft velvet caress

across her desiccated skin.
	Anchored by rhizoids
	this slithering layer

seeps out through pores,
	spreads like verdigris –
	a tight-fitting glove.

Around hair roots
	cerotodon begins, small and tight,
	and soon she is crowned

with a mass of fire –
	red and fertile in spots of light;
	orange embers glow under the forest canopy.

Liverwort breeds in the fossae above her clavicle
	and tracks towards marchantia in the jugular notch.
	Below, cladonia sprout their tiny

umbrella organs across her cleavage.
	Mood moss, wispy while dry
	is verdant and lush when moist

between her legs.
Spores spread.
She flourishes.

Her nails gleam
with gloss from the thorax of bluebottle.
Her black eyes

glisten, reflect the green sheen
of a magpie's nape.
Wet leaves around her grow cold,

slick in the shade. An odour of rot
from rank weeds touches the ends
of her olfactory nerves.

Her mouth waters.
She ripens
out of the Earth

as something   else.

Something   vivid

Sibyl of the cwm

staring eyes   soon be pecked out
ants tramp over rabbit head
trawl for morsels

stew was tasty
hot and hearty
keep me going long days

always put dead thing out there
sometimes neck-broken bird
or squirrel   fish carcass

rabbit head good decoy
keep nosy dogs out
cave   mine   no-one else

me here before made memory
many summers   not know count
or winters

only travel out in dark hours
forage in shadows
for collect water wild garlic in spring

horse parsley   chervil
in summer   sorrel dandelion and nettle
when shorter days come

berries nuts mushroom
some nights   in owl time
follow foxy mud path

to beach   for catch fish or crab
and swim

winter safer

people come warmer days
with dogs   children
then me spend longtime in cave

move small rocks
make false wall
crawl in back tunnel

wait where bats roost
sleep sound in dream-story
in warm smell of earth

and sometime
in daytime creep out
view people

some look here
stare at place where hide
high up   I see all steep valley

watch below
through ivy hanging trees.
Not see me.

Stillwatch

torn-clawed
torso twisted
air-still
flash-instant frozen
set to snap

sunslant clearing
soft underfoot
hazel, beech, oak
treefull leafworld

talons deep in her throat
fine fur scored
buzzard looks
eye to eye
liquid calm

killwatch

beak razors skin
slashes soft kitten belly
tears meat
viscera hangs red
over white pelt
ironblood scent

skillwatch

claws grasp furslack
wide wingpulse
air-rise
but her legs still run.

Becoming wolf

when winter night too cold
take wolf skin to wear,
become Mai-coh,
soft furdense
keep warm in deep frost, me

pads crunch on frozen leaves
heaped on woodland paths

stop, wait quiet, raise ears.

Air is ice in nose
breath cloudwhite,
but scents come clear

smoke of burning oakwood up valley
badger den across stream
smell of warm meat
cat scat, otter this way.

Sit quiet, listen.
Small things rustle in leaves
owl ruffles wings awake,
sea hits shore way below.

There!
Far off, very far
comes call from snow on high mountain
echo spreads warm in beating blood.

I raise head, open throat,
send cry back from forest
know will be heard on top crags
through frozen night.

Barn owl over Teifi marshes

I am white air
sailing over meadow
shadowless over reed beds

I lighten dusk
float in circles
fly-swoop to take prey.

And someone waits among bare trees
I fly towards her, straight and level
face to face

eye to eye as I pass
nothing to concern
I flow on, feathered mist

dissolving into twilight
and turn my attention
to night business

Tawny night

And nightly under the simple stars
As I rode to sleep the owls were
bearing the farm away
(Dylan Thomas, 'Fernhill')

In the dark silence of night
he calls
whew whew hoohooo

round tawny notes
I can almost touch.
He calls, she responds …

whew whew whew
hoohooohhooo
music of night forest and field edges

their cries sweep the day away
scoop me into the night
and lead me in twists and turns

among shadow trees
in woodland stillness
along the path to my place of sleep.

Mouldwarp*

Mole paw was charm
belong my mother
for ward off toothache.
Ha! Charm not work,
she no teeth when she die.
Me, not believe that magic.
My way different medicine,
with plants.

Mole hand left hanging
by cave door,
there many summers,
mother longtime in earth now,
body gone to soil.

One day, paw gone.

Look all around,
all over ground, not there.
No loss, no worry for old thing.

Next day, in topfield dawn
for gather mushroom.
Stretch back, look up –
new soil all over,
many little mountains across grass.
Me laugh.

Ha! Mole paw work,
he work hard.

**Middle English word for a mole.*

A god appears under the old apple tree

Slipfoot on deep ice.
Suck in longbreath of cold air.
Stop. Secure balance.

And he is there
red-pelted on white ground.
Clear eyes on me. Attentionful.

I swim in his amber gaze.
Wait, feel his wildness,
his in-the-moment dignity.

Stand before his all-seeing watchfulness.
I know he sees my wildness is lost
that my 'present' rests on my past

that I can connect with him
for only one instant
on this snowslope of sunglance.

My thought undoes me:
what happens next?
He turns, lopes away.

His bushtail bronze
brushed with silverlight
waves at my insufficiency.

Vriksasana

Feet sink into ground
earth crumbles between toes
dark and warm
mineral scents rise

as I soil-delve
beneath forest floor
where it's earthy, but not earthly.
How beautifully slow

our gradual growth
as we lumber our days,
our intertwined roots
foraging among foundations.

We measure seasons here
not days or hours.
My body extends in spring
lifts through the mid-line

centred and steady in the core
where energy moves up my long spine
and branches lengthen
as hands reach towards light

leaves tremble fresh green
flutter in morning air.
Fruits swell in summer days
as flesh ripens

roots plunge deeper
until the rains come
and we relax,
sap-slacken into lingering time.

We are steadfast in westerly gales
durable in north easterlies
as unhurried leaves become
russets and auburns

rustle, fall, fly
and our cells rest into the dark days
in the still of coldness
and unseen sleep.

Aspen tree
Populus tremula

Even when there is no wind
your movement draws me.
Always whispering the air
I rest beneath you
inhale the scent of grass
in warm Spring sun.
If I weren't here
would your leaves still quiver
on even the quietest days?

I came back to sit beneath
your shivering canopy
the film of a life flickering
frame by frame
in light against sky.
Remember that day
when I saw no point in me.
Is there an answer yet?

Lately I found you on another road
your leaves fluttering
above a foreign hillside.
I wonder at you
and see all of you tremble
and I know
that this
this
is all the reason I need.

Night in a beach cave

While I wait
grains of sand trickle over skin,

surround all my body.
As I sink into the hollow

rocks settle around me
and creak into comfy darkness.

Water bleeds from hanging walls
drips slow down slopes,

rock pleats into the push and shove
of sedimentary beds,

flow-folded plates
displaced into intense creases

of stress deformation, compaction.
A small fissure makes a flag of sky

as night edges away, grows colder
outside, waves thunder onto shore

and as I bury deeper
they shush and dispel to meet a horizon

where light catches sea breath.
At last, dawn arrives

sailing over the brink
to where I sigh in the dark.

Prayer to a stone

We mine you
carve you, smash you
make tools, bridges, walls

burial chambers, henges
monuments, weapons and jewels
birthstones   gravestones.

Pressed mud condensed
transformed into
your slabbed strength

split, cracked
erupted, fallen in pieces,
where now we watch

pebbles laden with minerals
rattle in sucking surf –
magical hagstone

to protect and heal,
snakeskin serpentinite
mottled with red,

mermaid's tears
green pebbles flecked with marble,
granite, slate, siltstone, flint

feldspar, quartz, coral,
mica, cornelian, amber, jet,
all the weight of the world

load of the Earth,
your heft in my hand.

Heart-shaped stones

They roll in on rumbling tides,
rest on flat sand

on the shore of dreaming
just above low water mark.

Some scramble in surf
like words tumbling in your brain,

become buried
just under the surface,

or many feet below.
They may be sucked out

to where dolphins feed and
leap, or settle on the line

that defines high tide.
You never know

quite where they will appear.
But keep looking,

always keep looking.
The surprise when you find one

is astounding.

Onward

Soft sand massages feet
cold cold sea laps seared skin
and salt seasons lips

at the world's wild edge
where lungs wrap around pure air
breathe all the way into toes.

Sun sparks on wave tops
light refractions weave gold below
while oystercatcher whistles coast over

a clear view to Ynys Enlli
across the wide of the bay;
and surf swells to lift

all the weight of the world's water
to carry me away